KT-225-177

Written by Jean-Pierre Verdet
Illustrated by Luc Favreau

Specialist adviser:
Jack Challoner, The Science Museum

ISBN 1 85103 174 X
First published 1993 in the United Kingdom
by Moonlight Publishing Ltd,
36 Stratford Road, London W8
Translated by Margaret Malpas

POCKET WORLDS

Understanding Light and Colour

Where do colours come from?

The world is full of colours.

It's the beginning of summer. Everything is bright. The trees are green, and there are flowers of every colour – red, blue, yellow, pink, purple, white, and even green. You can see brightly-coloured butterflies in the air.

But what happens in the evening? The sun sets, and all the colours fade. Have you heard people say that all cats are grey at twilight? It's true.

The light of the sun makes the colours in the world around us. On a clear, dry day the colours are much brighter than in damp misty weather.

It's dawn, the very beginning of the day. The air is full of tiny drops of water, which reflect the light. The sky looks white.

Now the warmth of the sun has dried the mist, and the sky is blue. But some fluffy white clouds are forming.

There's going to be a storm. The clouds cover the sun, and the sky grows dark. After the storm the sun comes out again.

A rainbow forms as sunlight bounces off raindrops. At sunset the sky looks red as the sun shines through dust above the horizon.

A blacksmith looks at the colour of the metal, and listens to the sound it makes, to tell him how hot the horseshoe is.

Light often comes from hot objects.

Anything will begin to glow when it is very hot – over 500 degrees centigrade. A piece of iron in a fire changes colour as it gets hotter. At first it turns a dull dark red, but at 1,000 degrees centigrade it becomes bright red. Never try to do this yourself, as you could burn yourself badly.

Before there was electric light, ordinary people used rush lights, which were reeds dipped in tallow (mutton fat). Richer people could afford wax candles. Both gave a gentle orange-yellow light.

Halogen lamps give a clear white light, because the filament in the bulb is very hot.

When iron is heated to 6,000 degrees centigrade, it changes colour from red to white. It becomes white hot. At night, when there is no natural light from the sun, we need artificial light. Most kinds of artificial light use heat to make light. People used to light their homes with candles of different kinds, or with lamps that burned oil or gas. The American scientist Edison made the first electric light bulb in 1879. Inside a bulb is a wire called a filament. When the light is switched on, this wire gets very hot (4,000 degrees centigrade) and glows brightly. Eventually the wire burns. This is what happens when a bulb blows. If you shake a light bulb which doesn't work any more, you can hear the broken wire rattling inside.

12

You can see hot objects such as light bulbs or the Sun because they give out their own light. Most things you can only see because they reflect light. Mirrors and shiny metals reflect most of the light that falls on them. Light travels through glass and transparent plastics. It also travels through steam and mist, though not so well.

Sunlight contains light of all the colours of the rainbow.

In 1666 Sir Isaac Newton showed what happens when ordinary white sunlight passes through a glass prism. You can see the colours on the screen in the picture. If you can find a prism at school, you can try this for yourself.

White light splits up into lots of different colours which always come in the same order: red at one end, and violet at the other. Beyond these colours are others (infrared and ultraviolet) which we can't see, but which some insects can.

What is light?

No-one knows exactly, but physicists know quite a lot about how it behaves.

Light is made up of waves.

When a beam of light meets an object which is not transparent, the object absorbs some of the light and reflects some of it.

The bird looks yellow because it reflects yellow light and absorbs light of any other colour. The blue flower reflects blue light and absorbs the rest. And so on.

White things absorb hardly any light, and reflect light of all colours. Black things absorb light of all colours, and reflect almost none.

When physicists studied the way in which light behaves, they realized that it must be made up of waves, just as sound is. Different colours of light have different wavelengths: red light has long waves (like low sounds), and violet light has short waves (like high sounds).

Light travels in straight lines.

Although light consists of waves, it sometimes behaves as though it was made of straight beams. When it is reflected off a mirror it travels straight. And look at the straw in the glass of water. It looks broken, because light travels differently through air and water.

Fireworks

The colour of a light doesn't always depend on the temperature of the object. If you very carefully sprinkle tiny grains of different substances into the flame of a bunsen burner, the flame will change colour for a moment as these metals and minerals burn. Always ask for the help of an adult with experiments like this one.

Fireworks contain gun-powder, of course, but their various colours come from other powders: zinc, copper, iron, salt and so on, which colour the flames as they burn.

The coloured flames in the picture below are all made by burning metals: sodium (yellow), strontium (orangey red), copper (blue-green) and potassium (mauve).

The centre of this painter's colour wheel is a triangle made up of the three colours: red, blue and yellow. The outside of the wheel shows the result of mixing paints of those colours. Green is made by mixing yellow and blue. Orange is made by mixing red and yellow. Purple is made by mixing red and blue. The colour wheel helps painters mix their colours.

All colours of paint from just three!

Painters have red, blue and yellow as their primary colours. By mixing them carefully, a painter can make most colours. Mixing all three together gives a muddy brown colour.

Remember how you can split white light, through a prism, into all the colours of the rainbow? Mix the three primary colours of light, and you have white light.

You can make white light from just three coloured lights, by shining them together. These three colours are red, green and blue, and are called the primary colours of light. Any colour can be made by adding the right amount of each of the primary colours together. Mixing any two primary-coloured lights makes complementary colours: cyan (blue plus green), magenta (red plus blue) and yellow (red plus green).

Coloured glass only lets through some of the colours of light shining on it. This is why it looks coloured. Blue glass lets through only blue light. Yellow glass lets through red and green light, but not blue light. Where different coloured glasses are placed together, they will often not let any light through, and they look black.

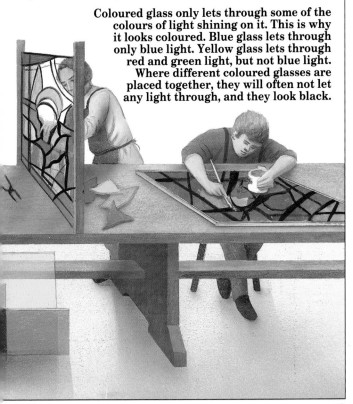

How does a painter choose his colours?

A painter works with coloured powders, not with lights. The powder is mixed with liquid, usually either oil or water, so that the artist can use a brush to put the paint on his picture. It is very important that the mixture is always the same. Here you can see the artist's assistant carefully grinding powder to make more paint.

Prehistoric people painted pictures on the walls of their caves

They used brown paints made from different kinds of earth, with white from chalk, and black from charcoal.

Icons are the holy pictures of Eastern Orthodox Christians.

Icons are painted on wood.

The artist mixes his paint with water and glue. Sometimes he may stick silver or gold leaf on to parts of the picture

Since the 17th century, most European painters have painted their pictures on canvas which has been soaked in a mixture of zinc oxide and glue and stretched on a wooden frame. This canvas is used for oil paints (powdered colours mixed with oil).

Nowadays we have all kinds of paints:

water-colours and poster paints for mixing
with water to paint on paper; oil paints
for painting on canvas; coloured pencils,
pastels and felt-pens for drawing on paper.

Acrylic paints are made of a mixture of resin
and water. The paint dries quickly as
the water evaporates, leaving a transparent
coloured film which is very strong
and doesn't get darker as it gets older.

Vincent van Gogh's palette

Musicians in Europe use only twelve different notes to write their music.

Painters use just a few different tubes of paint to make all their pictures.

You can recognize Vincent van Gogh's paintings (1) by their powerful style and colouring.

Paul Gauguin (2) painted large areas in single colours.

Paul Cézanne (3) composed much more complicated pictures, using subtle colours.

Georges Seurat (4) followed the ideas of the scientist Chevreul. Instead of mixing the colour he wanted on a palette, like most artists, he painted tiny dots of the colours that he would have mixed. When you look at a picture painted like this, your eye joins the dots together and mixes the colours.

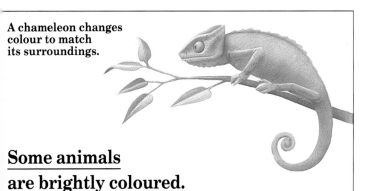
A chameleon changes colour to match its surroundings.

Some animals are brightly coloured.

Some need to merge into the background to escape from their enemies. They are camouflaged, like the chameleon.
Others want to scare their enemies by looking really dangerous, like the octopus.
A creature which is red may be trying to warn others that it is poisonous (like a ladybird). Some flies which can't sting look just like wasps, which can sting.

But some birds and animals seem to be brightly coloured just so that they can look beautiful, like this peacock.

An old-fashioned camera

Recording the colours of the natural world

For a long time scientists have known that some chemicals, such as silver chloride, turn black when light falls on them. In 1816 Nicéphore Niepce worked out how to use them to take black and white photographs.

In 1861 James Maxwell made the first colour photograph, by taking the same picture with three different films – each was sensitive to one primary colour.

A praxinoscope

The lens of a camera turns the image upside-down.

Moving pictures

Before the cinema was invented, it was possible to show pictures on a screen by using a magic lantern, which worked like a slide-projector. To see moving pictures you had to use machines like the praxinoscope, which showed a series of pictures taken one after the other. In the mid-19th century the Lumière brothers opened the first cinema, showing moving pictures.

Television pictures are made from little dots of light turning on and off on the screen.

The more dots there are, the closer together they are, and the sharper the picture looks. The faster they turn on and off, the less the picture flickers. The pictures on our TV screens change fifty times every second.

Lasers produce light of very pure colour.

The rays of light from a laser are so fine that they can travel a long way without spreading at all, so they don't get weaker at a distance, like an ordinary torch beam.

This laser produces a green beam. Astronomers aim it ten times a second at small mirrors on the surface of the moon and wait for the light to bounce back. By timing this, they can work out the distance   from the earth to the moon.

Colour printing

This book was printed with just four colours: yellow, magenta, cyan and black.

The printer needed to use black for the pictures as well as for the letters. The other 'colour' he used was the white of the paper. If a printer wants part of a picture to be pink, for example, he prints a sprinkling of red (magenta) dots on the white paper. For orange he uses thousands of little red dots mixed with thousands of yellow ones. Black dots close together make dark grey, and further apart they make a lighter grey. That's how four colours can make every colour you need.

If you look at this book through a good magnifying glass, you will be able to see the dots of colour.

The four primary colours for printing: black, cyan, magenta and yellow

Playing with light

Try making shadow puppets. Cut out some cardboard shapes of animals or people, and glue them on to sticks. Then use a torch to project their shadows on to a white wall. Or make shapes with your hands and see what their shadows look like; that way you can make moving pictures.

If you make a top like this and spin it, it will look white. Can you remember why?

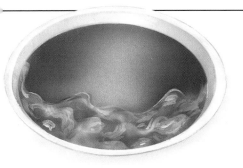

A rainbow on a plate

Take a soup plate, and put some water in it. Add a few drops of black ink, put the plate on a light windowsill (but not in bright sunlight). Put a drop of oil on the inky water, and you should see all the colours of the rainbow. You sometimes see this outside in the street, if some oil has fallen into a puddle of water.

Next time you blow soap bubbles, look at them carefully. You should see lots of colours in each one.

Index

Are you interested in these subjects?
There are lots more **Pocket Worlds**!